UNLOCKING THE MYSTERIES
OF THE
BIBLE

DEACON ALVIN BRAY

WALDENHOUSE PUBLISHERS, INC.
WALDEN, TENNESSEE

UNLOCKING THE MYSTERIES OF THE BIBLE

Copyright ©2018 William Alvin Bray. All rights reserved. No part of this book may be reproduced in any form or by any electronic or mechanical means including information storage and retrieval systems, without permission in writing from the copyright holders. The only exception is by a reviewer, who may quote short excerpts in a review.

Type and Design by Karen Paul Stone

Published by Waldenhouse Publishers, Inc.

100 Clegg Street, Signal Mountain, Tennessee 37377 USA

888-222-8228   www.waldenhouse.com

ISBN: 978-1-947589-03-2

Library of Congress Control Number: 2018904247

Presents selections of scriptures from the King James version of the Bible with some popular biblical stories clarified. In a search for more truth, information from *The Lost Books of the Bible* is also included in a discussion of material omitted from the King James version. One illustration. -- Provided by publisher.

REL070000 Religion : Christianity - General

REL006000 Religion : Biblical Studies - General

REL006050 Religion : Biblical Commentary - General

DEDICATION

In loving memory of my parents,
Elder Lefes and Annie Mae (Phillips) Bray
And dearly beloved brother
James Lepharis Bray (Fu Fu)
You will always be cherished in my thoughts,
mind and heart.

CONTENTS

Abraham and Sarah / Ishmael /
  Abraham, Isaac and Jacob   7

Joseph and His Brothers   9

Joseph Sold into Egypt/Put in Prison   15

Pharaoh Puts His Chief Baker and
  Butler in Prison   17

Pharaoh's Dream / Joseph Interprets   19

Concerning Joseph's Bones   21

Jesus – Mother / Parents   23

Jesus – Brothers and Sisters   25

The Baptism   27

Difference Between the Bibles –
  Douay Rheims and the King James   29

Who Was Melchizedek   31

The Three Wise Men   33

Hidden History   35

What Belongs to Caesar / What Belongs to God   37

The Philistines' Unbelief   41

Hot Topics   43

    A) Catholics Worship Mary

    B) Extra Books of Daniel

    C) The Thirteenth Chapter

    D) Ten Lepers Healed

    E) The Theme of the 23rd Psalms

The Fig Tree / The Forbidden Fruit   51

Your thoughts – Your Opinions   53

SPECIAL NOTICE

Some of these writings one may find hard to believe, or hard to swallow, but take it with a grain of salt. It is true. The Bible has a lot of history. Everything has not been told.

CHAPTER ONE
Abraham and Sarah

Abraham was the father of all nations. God told Abraham and Sarah that he would bless them. They were going on 10 years in the land. Sarah asked her husband, "I thought you said the Lord was going to bless us. We have been here almost 10 years and we have no kids" (paraphrased). Sarah no doubt said, "Maybe it's your fault," and Abraham said, "How do you know it's not your fault?" This is when Sarah gave her maid, Hagar, to be Abraham's wife, and Hagar conceived a child, and Sarah was very angry. But this was all in God's plans.

Ishmael

Ishmael was Abraham's son by his maid. Her name was Hagar (Gen. 16:8-11). The Bible states that Ishmael would multiply. Also, the Bible says Ishmael would be a madman (Gen. 17:10-12) and his hand would be against every man, and every man's hand against him. Ishmael had 12 princes. One of Ishmael's daughters married Esau (Gen. 28:9). Ishmael's daughter's name was Mahalath.

Ishmael also had 12 sons, but you do not see much mention about his sons. It is as though the writer omitted this information. His sons were named Nebaioth, Kedar, Abdeel, Mibsam, Mishma, Dumah, Massa, Hadad, Tema, Jefur, Naphish and Kedemah.

Ishmael and the 12 princes are the Arab side of the family.

The writers of the Bible put in what they wanted, and left out a lot. Why? They did not want the truth out. There are other important sources that they left out also.

The Bible has gone through several changes. It goes back to John Wycliffe, then William Tyndale. For some reason the writer wanted to keep the real truth hidden. But the Bible says everything that was kept hidden before the foundation of the world would be brought forth. The secret will be unveiled.

The Bible says that the first shall be last and the last shall be first. Everybody has a different opinion of what this means. What's your meaning of this saying? There is something else that has been disputed! Or covered up!

Abraham, Isaac and Jacob

Isaac was 40 years old when he took Rebekah for his wife (Genesis 25:20). She was the sister of Laban.

When Rebekah became pregnant, she didn't know that she was having twins. The children began to struggle within her womb. She decided to go to the Lord to find out what was happening. The Lord told her that she was having two nations (twins). The Lord told her, "The elder shall serve the younger."

When it was time for the twins to be born, the Bible said Esau came out first. Then Jacob grabbed Esau's heel and came out second. In Biblical times, the oldest became the beneficiary of the family inheritance. Deep down in Rebekah's heart, she felt that by Jacob's grabbing Esau's heel, he was supposed to be the first born. During the time the boys were growing up, Rebekah still had in her heart that Jacob was supposed to have been the first born. Esau was a hunter, a man of the field, and Jacob was a dealer in tents. As the boys grew, their father was old and about to move on (about ready to die). He called Esau in so that he could pass the blessing on to him.

Now Isaac's wife Rebekah was eavesdropping while Isaac was talking to Esau. Isaac wanted Esau to make him his favorite stew. When Esau went to hunt, his mother heard the conversation and she knew this was the time to deceive her husband.

She told Jacob to go and get a goat. She prepared a stew for Jacob to give to his father. Jacob said, "Mama, I am not hairy like Esau." His mother told him not to worry about it, because she would put some goat hair on Jacob's arm and around his neck. She prepared the stew for Isaac. And Isaac said, "You sound like Jacob, but you feel like Esau." So, Isaac ate the stew and bestowed the blessing on Jacob.

As one looks back closely, this had to be in God's plans. Now when you go back, when the people of Israel were going against God's law, the Lord would let another nation put them in check. The Lord was the same back then and is the same today.

God is still in control. When Isaac died and was buried, Rebekah sent Jacob to her brother's house to get away from Esau. She thought that Esau would try to harm his brother, Jacob.

Jacob stayed with Laban close to twenty years. While there, Jacob worked for seven years to earn

Rachel's hand in marriage. But Laban played a trick on Jacob and gave Leah to Jacob for his wife. When Jacob arose the next morning he realized that Laban had tricked him. Jacob was upset. The custom was that the youngest wasn't supposed to get married before the oldest.

So Jacob agreed to work for another seven more years for Rachel. The other seven years went by in a breeze. Then Jacob worked six more years for the herd. The Lord blessed Jacob.

Jacob had twelve sons, the twelve tribes of Israel, and Jacob had one daughter name Dinah. Laban changed Jacob's wages several times. Jacob and Laban's children couldn't quite get along. So Jacob took his two wives and children and left. When Laban came back, he found out that Jacob and his family had left. This upset Laban, and he went looking for Jacob and his grandchildren. On his way the Lord spoke to Laban and said, "Don't cause any harm to Jacob."

Laban was also upset because his idol was taken. Rachel had it hidden in her saddle bag, but Laban didn't find it.

Rachel asked her father to forgive her because she couldn't come down off the beast (a camel or a donkey) because it was that time of season. So Laban and Jacob made a peace treaty.

CHAPTER TWO

Joseph and His Brothers

Joseph had a chosen mission that was in God's plan for his life. Joseph's father was Jacob. Joseph had 11 other brothers and a sister. His brothers were Reuben, Simeon, Levi, Judah, Zebulun, Issachar, Dan, Gad, Asher, Naphtali, and Benjamin (Genesis 49:1-28). These were the 12 tribes of Israel. Joseph also had one sister. Her name was Dinah (Genesis 34:1-8).

Joseph's brothers hated him because their father loved him more. Jacob would send his sons out to tend to the herd. No doubt, some of his brothers would not do their share of the work, and Joseph would report it to their father. Joseph would have dreams and told his brothers about them. The brothers did not receive the dreams too well. It also upset Joseph's father (Genesis 37).

As time went on, Jacob was making a coat of many colors. Jacob sent Joseph's brothers to tend to the herds, and Joseph was told to stay so his father could see if the coat would fit. As soon as the brothers got out of sight, they talked among themselves. They discussed how they could do what they wanted, and they didn't have to worry about Joseph telling on them.

But everything that took place was in God's plan. Instead of tending to the herds, they decided to go to Dothan, and their father finished the coat for Joseph. Joseph tried the coat on, and it was a perfect fit. Jacob began to worry about his sons. They had been gone quite a while, so he sent Joseph to look for them. Joseph looked for them, no doubt calling each one by his name, but he got no answer. Soon he met a man who asked him who he was looking for. The man was an angel of God. He told Joseph that he heard the brothers say they were going into the city. Joseph made his way to Dothan calling out their names along the way.

As he traveled about he called out, "Levi, Reuben, where are you?" He went further into the land calling out for his brothers. His brothers saw him on the horizon and trembled in fear.

No doubt they were saying amongst themselves, "Here comes that dreamer; we will be in a lot of trouble." So, they plotted to kill him.

But Reuben said, "We shouldn't harm him because the blood will be on our hands."

Joseph's brothers came up with a plan. When Joseph reached them they would grab him and take off his coat and put him in a pit. They killed a goat and ripped Joseph's coat and dipped it in the goat's blood. They then traveled a few feet and sat down to eat. Joseph called out to his brothers over and over again. They pretended not to hear him, and instead ignored him.

During that time a company of Ishmaelites were going down to Egypt. They heard Joseph calling out from the pit. There were Midianites traveling the road too. They heard Joseph's cries, and they drew him out of the pit and sold him to the Ishmaelites (Genesis 37).

Joseph's brothers did not sell him as people were led to believe.

When Reuben went to check on Joseph, he called out to Joseph, and he didn't get an answer. Reuben looked into the pit and Joseph was not in the pit. Then Reuben went back to his brothers and told them he could not find Joseph. So the brothers took Joseph's coat, ripped it, and put the blood of a goat on it and took it back to their father.

Remember, this was all in God's plan for Joseph. God had already told Abraham before, "I will bless you, but your descendants will be in bondage for 400 years." God was preserving the children of Israel.

SELF-PRONOUNCING EDITION.

In Which all the Proper Names are Divided, Accented, and Marked with the Vowel Sounds, Showing how they should be Pronounced.

Trade

COMBINATION

Mark.

HOLY BIBLE

SHOWING IN SIMPLE FORM ALL CHANGES, ADDITIONS AND OMISSIONS THAT APPEAR IN
THE REVISED VERSION, ENABLING ALL BIBLE READERS TO SEE AT
A GLANCE WHEREIN THE TWO VERSIONS DIFFER.

CONTAINING

The Old and New Testaments.

TRANSLATED OUT OF THE ORIGINAL TONGUES,

AND

WITH THE FORMER TRANSLATIONS DILIGENTLY COMPARED AND REVISED.

CONFORMABLE TO THE EDITION OF 1611, COMMONLY KNOWN
AS THE AUTHORIZED OR KING JAMES VERSION

COPIOUS MARGINAL REFERENCES, CHRONOLOGICAL TABLES AND MANY IMPORTANT AND VALUABLE AIDS TO THE
STUDY OF THE HOLY SCRIPTURES. WRITTEN TO INCREASE THE INTEREST AND SIMPLIFY THE WORD OF GOD

LIGHT OF THE WORLD

CHAPTER THREE

Joseph Sold into Egypt

Joseph sold to Potiphar, an officer of Pharaoh (Genesis 39)

God was with Joseph, and everything that Joseph did the Lord let him prosper. As time went on, Potiphar's wife tried to get Joseph to sleep with her, but he declined. This behavior went on day in and day out. Joseph still did not give in to her desires.

More details about this are found in the book of Jasher. This book was kept out of the Bible. As a matter of fact, there are more books that were not entered into the King James Bible. You will hear preachers say you don't add or take away from the Bible. Well this was practiced way back then. The Bible has been revised several different times. The illustration on the facing page shows evidence of the beginning of the additions, omissions and changes.

Getting back to Joseph's story and Potiphar's wife, her name was Zelieah. Again, the Book of Jasher will give more details about several subjects that were left out of the Bible. The mention about the Book of Jasher is found in II Samuel 1:1-18. As follow:

The 18th verse also bade them to teach the children of Judah the use of the bow; "behold, it is written in the Book of Jasher." Another reverence is Joshua 10:13. Everything is still going according to God's plan. God knows everyone's beginning and everyone's ending.

Zelieah tempted Joseph over and over to no avail. Zelieah kept on. This time she sent two men, Pharaoh's officers the cupbearer and the chief baker. They were assigned as guard duty and supposed to be on their post at all times, rain, sleet or snow. However, Potiphar's wife sent everyone out.

She beautified herself by putting on eyeshadow, lip gloss, and outlined her lips. So, when Joseph came in to do his chores, she grabbed him. Joseph did a quarterback sneak and ran from her presence naked. When Potiphar came back, she told him a lie about Joseph and showed him Joseph's coat. More details about this are in the book of Jasher.

Potiphar got really angry and had Joseph put in prison, but God was with him, and the Lord let him prosper. He was placed as warden in the prison. Everything he did, the Lord let him prosper. He would get the prisoners up to go to work on detail duty. This went on for a season.

God put another piece of the puzzle together. At this time Potiphar couldn't sleep thinking about the incident that took place about his wife. Potiphar was Pharaoh's chariot driver. Every morning Potiphar would suit up and pick up Pharaoh. They would travel the land together. One particular time Potiphar came up late, and Pharaoh said to Potiphar, "The last couple of days you have been late. The quicker we go out, the quicker we get back." Potiphar told Pharaoh that every since this incident about his wife and Joseph, he toiled all night, and when he finally got to sleep, he wound up oversleeping.

CHAPTER FOUR

Pharaoh Put the Chief Baker
and Butler in Prison

Pharaoh told Potiphar that he would check into this when they got back. So, when they got back, Pharaoh called the chief baker and the cupbearer. He inquired about the incident with them both.

He asked them could they confirm or deny the incident. And they both said, "Pharaoh, we don't know."

Pharaoh got mad and said, "What do you mean, you don't know? You're supposed to always be on your post, rain or shine." They told Pharaoh that Potiphar's wife had made everyone leave their posts, and they did not have a choice but to leave. Pharaoh got mad at their response and had them both put in prison. They were put in prison where Joseph was in charge.

As time went by, every morning Joseph would have a roll call. He got the prisoners up to go to work detail. This went on a couple of weeks. Then one day Joseph went to get the prisoners up. Joseph noticed the cupbearer and the chief baker were looking confounded. Joseph asked them why they looked so confounded. The cupbearer told Joseph he had had a dream. Joseph told him that God was the interpreter of all dreams, so the cupbearer told Joseph his dream. The Lord revealed the dream to Joseph, and he told the meaning of the dream to the cupbearer. Joseph told him that in three days Pharaoh would send some men to get him and put him back to his former job.

This sounded good! So, when the chief baker heard the good outcome, he was happy and made a gesture to Joseph. He told Joseph that he too had had a dream. The chief baker told Joseph his dream, but Joseph's interpretation did not have a good ending. Joseph told the chief baker that in three days Pharaoh would send men to get him out, and hang him from a tree. No doubt the chief baker probably said to himself, "Maybe I should have kept my mouth shut."

The Bible states that in three days it was Pharaoh's birthday, and both men's dream came true. When they were released, Joseph said, "Don't forget to mention me."

CHAPTER FIVE

Pharaoh's Dream / Joseph Interprets

A couple of seasons went by, and God put another piece of the puzzle into play. This time Pharaoh had a dream that puzzled him. Pharaoh called on all the magicians and wise men throughout Egypt. He told them about his dream. He promised that whoever could interpret his dream would get a position. Of all the magicians in the 129 Provinces, no one could interpret Pharaoh's dream. The men were gathered in a corner going over Pharaoh's dream. Pharaoh called out to them, "Have you come up with the meaning?"

The men shouted, "Not yet, King Pharaoh!"

Pharaoh's patience began to wear thin. Pharaoh, no doubt, said, "In other times you would rattle the dream in a snap."

About that time the cupbearer said, "Oh, King Pharaoh! I know a man that can tell you the meaning of the dream." The cupbearer reminded King Pharaoh that about two years before he had gotten mad at the cupbearer and the chief baker for not being on their posts concerning the allegation about Potiphar's wife. Pharaoh had both men thrown in prison because they weren't on their posts. The cupbearer reminded the King of how Joseph had interpreted their dreams and how they had come true.

So Pharaoh sent for Joseph. Joseph shaved and came before King Pharaoh. Pharaoh began to tell Joseph his dream, and the Lord revealed Pharaoh's dream to Joseph. And Pharaoh gave Joseph another name, Zaphnath-Paaneah, and gave him a wife named Asenath, who was the daughter of Potiphar's priest of On.

All this was still going according to God's plan. Little by little, piece by piece, God was putting it in place to save his people, the people of Israel.

When Joseph became governor, a famine had come to all the people in the 129 Provinces. They had spent all their money and traded their herds and land. They had nothing left but themselves. They had gotten rid of everything they owned, and this is how all the people came to Egypt, and when they started on their 400 years that the Lord told Abraham.

During this time Joseph's whole family came to Egypt and were in bondage for 400 years. While Joseph was in Egypt, two of his sons were born. Joseph was 30 years old (Genesis 41-46). His firstborn was Manasseh, and his second born was Ephram.

Joseph's brothers did not know that he was governor of Egypt. Joseph made it known to them that he was governor.

CHAPTER SIX

Concerning Joseph's Bones

When the children of Israel's time was winding up, Joseph gave strict orders that when he died they should take his bones with them. Joseph saw Ephram's children to the third generation (Genesis 50:24). Surely God would visit them. When Joseph died he was 110 years old. They embalmed him and put him in a coffin. They didn't bury him because they were told to carry his bones when they left Egypt. Now Joseph's bones would be carried to the Promised Land.

The people, being hardheaded, spent 40 years wandering around in the wilderness. The Bible states that the children of Israel wandered in the wilderness for 40 years. From the 20-year-old to the oldest, all died in the wilderness except for two.

During this time Moses mentioned taking Joseph's bones with them (Exodus 13:19). As is known, the Bible is not in order, but here a little and there a little (Numbers 14:29-37).

Of all the people that were in Egypt, only the young ones, Joshua, the son of Nun, and Caleb, the son of Jephunneh, were left. The reason Joshua and Caleb were left is because they knew what was supposed to happen to Joseph's bones. The younger generation would have buried Joseph's bones on the way. They would have questioned why they were carrying this dead man's bones with them. They would have buried Joseph's bones in the wilderness. Joshua and

Caleb lived because they knew that Joseph's bones were supposed to be placed in the Promised Land.

In II Kings, Chapter 13: Verse 21, it is written that while Joshua and Caleb carried Joseph's coffin, they looked up and spied a band of men. One Bible called them the raiders; another Bible version called them Moabites. Now when you go back to the Book of Genesis, the Moabites and the Ammonites were Abraham's, Nephew's (Lot's) side of the family.

In the Book of Deuteronomy, the Lord told the children of Israel not to fight the Moabites, because the Moabites saw what happened when Joshua and Caleb threw Joseph's body down. As the bones of his body touched Elisha's body, Joseph's body came back to life. However, Joshua and Caleb had taken off, and they did not see this event (miracle). The Moabites saw it, and that is how it was known. Now later they had to fight the Moabites. Everything that happened was in God's plan. God is still in charge – today, yesterday and forever more.

CHAPTER SEVEN

Jesus – Mother / Parents

Jesus' mother, Mary.

Mary's parents are not mentioned in the Bible. There is one event located in Luke 2:36. This was Mary's mother.

Now Mary's parents are listed in the Lost Book of the Bible. I don't call it the Lost Book, because if something was lost, it would still be lost. So, in other words, the book is known as the Hidden Book! Perhaps a book that they did not want out.

Well here goes, if you want to know, from *The Lost Books of the Bible* by William Hone. Mary's parents were similar to Samuel's parents. Mary's father's name was Joachim, and her mother's name was Anna. Anna prayed to the Lord for a child, and she made a vow that she would dedicate the child to the Lord. The Lord granted her heart's desire.

When the child was weaned, Anna took her to the temple. Now there were others like Mary who were taken to the temple. There were 7 or 8 more virgins. Now, remember there were 12 tribes of Israel. So the other 7 or 8 virgins went to the temple and were taught. The temple was like a school building in our time.

When they turned 12 years old, they were supposed to go back to their tribe (city) and get married. Back then when a person turned 12 years old, they were considered grown, and when the time came for them to go back to their home, they were to get married. The priest told them it was time for the children to pay their vow.

Mary told the priest that she was going to stay a virgin for the Lord. The priest was shocked. His name was Issachar, one of the twelve of Israel. This was the custom of their country. When Mary said that she would stay a virgin for the Lord, the priest went to the leader to figure out what to do. They insisted he go to the Ark and inquire of the Lord. The Lost Book is a must for everyone to read. It will give you information that was left out of the Bible.

CHAPTER EIGHT

Jesus – Brothers and Sisters

Fast forward

Joseph, who was Jacob's son, guess what? He is the same Joseph that married Mary. God had everything mapped out according to his plan from the beginning. We go back to Genesis, where Pharaoh named Joseph Zaphnathpaaheah. Now when we venture into the New Testament, a lot of scholars do not seem to know, or do not get it. God gives you knowledge above college.

Now in the New Testament, Joseph was the same Joseph who was Jacob's son. In the New Testament Joseph goes by the name "Zebedee", a nick name for Joseph. Now let's travel to Matthew 4:21, and going on from thence, "Jesus saw two brethren [brothers], James the son of Zebedee [Joseph], and John, his brother, in a ship with Zebedee, their father, mending their net; and he [Jesus] called them." Now when Jesus was going about choosing his disciples, four of the disciples were his brothers (Matthew 13:55): James, John, Simon Peter, Judas. John AKA, Joses, and also known as Joseph.

In other words, Jesus' step father, Joseph, named one of his sons Joseph (Luke 5:10). Now when Jesus went to the mountain, he took three of his disciples, Peter, James and John. They were Jesus' close disciples. Also, they were his brothers (half brothers). Jesus had two sisters that you do not hear preachers talk about. As one will find in Mark 15:40, Mary

Magdalene and Salome were Jesus' half sisters (Mark 16:1). And when Jesus went to the mountain to pray, he took his brothers, Peter, James and John. (Matthew 13:55, 56).

CHAPTER NINE

The Baptism

Some preachers still have the baptism up in the air. The Bible says Jesus gave Peter the keys to the kingdom of heaven. In Acts 2:38, Peter said unto them all, "Repent and be baptized each of you in the name of Jesus Christ for the remission of sins, and you shall receive the gift of the Holy Ghost." That is like if I told you I was getting a truck, well there are all kinds of trucks. If I told you I was getting a Ford or a Chevy, you know what kind of truck I am getting.

It is better to be baptized right, being baptized in Jesus Christ's name. It is better to know that you know. This is a declared statement. The Bible did not say you might be saved. It said you shall be saved. So, if you are in doubt about your baptism, it is better to know if you were baptized in Jesus Christ's name. One, or two, baptisms won't hurt you. If anything, it will surely help you.

When the feast of the Passover drew near, Jesus knew it was time for him to go back to the Father. He called his disciples together after the feast. Jesus began to wash his disciples' feet (John 13:1-15). This was symbolic for their baptism. Jesus told his disciples, "What I do thou knowest not now, but thou shalt know hereafter" (John 13:7). "Beware of false prophets, dressed up as sheep, but down under they are raging wolves" (Matt. 7:15).

When Jesus came into the coast of Caesarea, he asked his disciples, "Who do men say that I, the son of man, am?" (Matt. 16:13-19).

Peter said, "Thou art the Christ, the son of the living God." Jesus told Peter this was revealed to Peter by the Father which is in heaven.

Jesus baptized only his disciples (John 4:1-3). When Jesus and his disciples were going to Gethsemane, there was a young man that followed Jesus and his disciples. He was the one that saw and heard Jesus' prayer. This man was John Mark (Mark 14:51-53).

CHAPTER TEN

Difference between the Bibles

1) Douay Rheims Bible

In The Douay Rheims Bible, the Book of Esther has 16 chapters; the Book of Daniel has 14 chapters. It has the book of I and II Machabees. There are books that the King James does not have. It has Tobias and Judith. The 23rd Psalm is the 22nd Psalm.

2) King James Bible

In The King James Bible, the Book of Esther has 10 chapters; the Book of Daniel has 12 chapters. It does not have the Machabees, Judith or Tobias.

There are also other books?

The Apocrypha Books.

CHAPTER ELEVEN
Who Was Melchizedek?

Melchizedek was Jesus Christ in the spirit form. He helped Abram fight the King of Sodom when they captured Lot, who was Abram's (Abraham's) nephew, not Abraham's brother (Genesis 14:18-21).

Lot's father was Haran (Genesis 11:31). Other references, Psalms 110:4; Hebrews 5:6-10; Hebrews 6:20; Hebrews 7:1-21.

The Bible says the King of Peace, King of Salem, without father, without mother, without descent, having neither beginning of days, nor end of life. (Hebrews 7:1-3).

Melchizedek and Yeshua.

Another mystery of the Bible is whether Melchizedek and Yeshua are the same person. Just who is Melchizedek? According to research, some say he is Jesus; others say he is the archangel Michael; while others say he could be Shem, the son of Noah. There are several clues in the Bible.

Melchizedek (Melkhey-Tsedek) is translated as King of Righteousness.

One will find Melchizedek in Genesis 14: "And Melchizedek, king of Salem, brought out bread and wine; now he was a priest of God Most High. And he blessed him and said, 'Blessed be Abram of God Most High, possessor of heaven and earth; and blessed be God Most High, who had delivered your enemies into your hand'." (Genesis 14:18-20).

Abraham felt compelled to give a tithe of all his possessions he got in battle to Melchizedek. Melchizedek must have been special to Abraham.

One will also find Melchizedek mentioned in Psalm 110:4. "The Lord hath sworn, and will not repent. Thou are a priest forever after the order of Melchizedek." (KJV) Melchizedek is referred to as a priest in this scripture.

CHAPTER TWELVE
The Three Wise Men

Three wise men went looking for the new born king (Jesus). Tradition has accorded names to these wise men: 1) Melkon, King of Persia, 2) Balthazar, a King of Arabia, and 3) Casper, a King of India.

Arabia was one of the earliest colonies of the ancient Cushite Empire of Biblical Ethiopia (present day Sudan). The Bible does not say what happened to John the Baptist when Herod was killing all the boy babies aged two on down, but there is a book that tells what happened to John. The Bible says John's father, Zacharias, was killed at the altar. But it does not say why.

When Herod's men found Zacharias, they slew him (Matt. 23:35), because he did not tell them where his son, John, was. He did not know. There are books that say what happened to John. It says that John's mother, Elisabeth, (reference St. Luke 1:5-6) picked up John and ran to the mountain. It was too high to climb. Well, God sent an angel, and the angel parted the mountain, and Elisabeth and her son were provided protection between the mountains. Elisabeth was the daughter of Aaron.

CHAPTER THIRTEEN

Hidden History

The Bible says no one had seen Jesus. From the original *African Heritage Study Bible* / King James Version. The footnote states: "As early as the Byzantine Period, the Greek Orthodox Church recast the Madonna as a Greek, and other European countries followed a similar practice. During the European Renaissance, Michelangelo (1475-1564) saw no problem in creating biblical characters as Italians without any concern for historical accuracy."

In other words, the paintings by Michelangelo showing Jesus and his disciples throughout the ages are misleading.

Michelangelo was an Italian Renaissance sculptor, painter, architect and poet. He was born in Caprese, Tuscany.

On your cell phone or tablet, pull up the following two words:

1. Greek Icon
2. Russian Icon

Jesus was a Jew (John 4:9). The Samaritans did not have any dealings with the Jews. The same thing is going on around the world today. People of different races cannot get along together. Beware lest any man spoil you through philosophy and vain deceit (Colossians 2:8).

CHAPTER FOURTEEN

What Belongs to Caesar / What Belongs to God

The officials were trying to stir up trouble. They went to Jesus trying to trap him. But Jesus knew their hearts. They brought up about the tithe (Matt. 22:18-22). Jesus said, "Render to Caesar what belongs to Caesar, and what belongs to God to God." God was concerned about salvation. Man has taken the word of God and put a twist on it.

The Bible says the Lord sends rain on the just and on the unjust alike. A lot of preachers are using God's message for material gain and profit.

Caesar is the name of a Roman family prominent from the Third Century B.C. The leaders were trying to stir up trouble (Matt. 22:17). Jesus knew their thoughts.

God is more concerned about people getting salvation and getting baptized in the name of Jesus Christ for remission of sin. The people were trying to trap Jesus, but it did not work. (Matt. 17:24-27)

When Peter and Jesus were traveling, the priest asked Peter, "Does your master pay tribute?"

And Peter said, "Yes." But Jesus rebuked Peter for his answer. He told Peter to go to the sea and the first fish he caught to take the coin from its mouth to pay the tribute money. Now Jesus rebuked Peter for his answer because Jesus did not want to offend the Jews (Matt.17:24-27; Luke 23:2).

The Bible says in Second Corinthians 9:6, "He that soweth sparingly shall reap also sparingly; but he which soweth bountifully shall reap also bountifully. Let every man give as he is able."

You know people say a lie will hurt. Guess what? The truth will also hurt. First Timothy 6, verse 10 says, "For the love of money is the root of all evil; which while some coveted after, they have erred from the faith and pierced themselves through with many sorrows."

The Bible says be not deceived (Gal. 6:7). "God is not mocked: for whatsoever a man soweth, that shall he also reap."

The Bible says (I Peter 5:2), "Feed the flock of God which is among you. Taking the oversight thereof, not by constraint, but willingly; not for filthy lucre, but of a ready mind." Now going back to the last prophet in the Old Testaments whose name was Malachi, all during the Old Testaments, the children of Israel would bring bad animals as a sacrifice unto the Lord. The Lord took care of the children of Israel and brought them out of bondage. The people started to bring polluted animals, some lame, sickly, and diseased, to sacrifice to the Lord. Instead of bringing first quality, they kept the good for themselves and brought the rejected animals to the Lord.

The Lord was displeased with this. The Lord told Malachi (Malachi 3:8) that the people were robbing God by bringing diluted offerings to the Lord.

Now, when Jesus Christ came on the scene, Jesus suffered and shed his blood for all mankind, for those who accepted him as their Lord and Savior. This did away with the animal sacrifice once and for all.

But most preachers go back to the Old Testaments and bring this out to the forefront saying, "Would a man rob God?" (Malachi 2:8). All mankind should worship the Lord from their hearts and not by lip service. The Lord knows those who are his, and the ones that are doing his will and keeping his commandments.

CHAPTER FIFTEEN
The Philistines' Unbelief

When Eli's two sons abused their authority, a man of God came to Eli and told him about his sons' behavior. Instead of Eli removing them from their position, he just talked to them, and kept them in charge of the ark (I Samuel 2:22-25).

During this time Elkanah and his wife, Hannah, prayed to the Lord for a child. She made a vow that she would give him to the Lord. Her prayer was answered, and when Samuel was weaned, Hannah dedicated him to the Lord.

The Lord called Samuel three times. Samuel thought that it was Eli that called him. The Lord told Samuel to warn Eli about his sons' behavior. The Lord stirred up the Philistines, and they fought against Israel. They lost a lot of soldiers including Eli's two sons, Hophni and Phinehas (I Samuel 4:4).

The Philistines went to battle with Israel. They killed Eli's two sons and captured the ark and brought it to their territory. The ark brought havoc to the five cities of the Philistines. The Philistines did not believe that God was fighting for the people of Israel. They thought it was a coincidence. In the five cities where the ark came, the men died and were smitten with tumors (I Samuel 5:12).

This happened in five cities. The ark was in their land for seven months. The five cities were Ashdod, Gaza, Askelon, Gath and Ekron. All of the priests of the cities came together and asked, "What shall we do?" So they made a new cart and got two cows that had calves. They locked up the calves because the Philistines still did not believe the Lord was fighting for the people of Israel.

The Philistines said if they put the calves up, they knew the cows would not leave their babies, but they were wrong. They followed the ark and the Bible said that the cows did not turn to the left or the right. Nor did they turn to go back to their calves. Finally, the Philistines knew without a shadow of a doubt that the Lord truly was fighting for the people of Israel (I Samuel 6).

HOT TOPICS

Catholics Worship Mary

The Catholics worship and praise Mary, the mother of our Lord and Savior. The reason the Catholic faith praises Mary is because when Jesus was a baby he performed several miracles. Even as a child Jesus performed miracles. But instead of giving honor where honor was due, the people gave praise to Mary. They knew Mary was the mother of our Lord and Savior. Mary was in the upper room with the other 120 people. Mary did not die for our sins. Jesus, her son, died for all mankind.

The Romans believe and worship Mary. The Pope cannot forgive man from their sins. The Lord Jesus is the only one who can forgive man from their sins.

The Lord knew all this would take place. The Bible says let the wheat and tares grow together. The Lord will be the one, and the only one, who will separate them. The wheat and tares are none other than the good and the bad. John told the people that came to be baptized that there was one that cometh after him who would be mightier than himself (Matthew 3:11-13; Luke 3:17).

All the miracles that Jesus did when he was a child are mentioned in the Lost Books of the Bible. I do not call it the "Lost." If something was lost, it would still be lost. In other words, they were hidden books that were omitted from the Bible. The Bible says things that were kept secret shall be revealed.

The Word of God is quick, and powerful, and sharper than any two edged sword (Hebrews 4:12).

Extra Books of Daniel

There is more on Daniel. Daniel had been in the Lion's den. Daniel interpreted Nebuchadnezzar's dream. He also interpreted the handwriting on the wall for Nebuchadnezzar's son. When King Nebuchadnezzar died, his son ruled. Belshazzar was Nebuchadnezzar's son.

The most important thing that Daniel did was he was the one who saved Mary's mother, Anna, from being stoned to death. This story is found in the thirteenth and fourteenth chapter of Daniel. These two chapters were left out of the King James version. There are other books that are not printed in the King James Bible. The King James Bible just carries the twelfth chapter.

The Thirteenth Chapter

There was a man named Joakim, and he took a wife whose name was Susanna (Anna). She was the daughter of Helcias and a very beautiful woman, and one who feared God. Her parents, being just, had instructed their daughter according to the Law of Moses. Joakim was very rich and had an orchard near his house. There were two agents that were appointed judges. Both men were in love with Anna. They tried to get her to lie with them. She refused and they both lied because she wouldn't sleep with them. They falsely accused her before the council. They thought because she refused their advances that she should be stoned to death for adultery. But their plan was foiled.

The Lord spoke to Daniel, and the spirit was upon him. He interrogated the men separately. Each man gave a different account of what happened. Daniel had convinced them of false witness by their own mouths. To fulfill the Law of Moses, both men were put to death, and innocent blood was saved on that day.

That was how Mary's mother, Anna, was saved. There is another scene concerning the temple of Bel and the dragon. Helcias and his wife praised God for their daughter Susanna (Anna) with Joakim her husband. For there was no dishonesty found in her, and Daniel became great in the sight of the people from that day and then forward.

Daniel was the King's guest (Daniel 14th Chapter) and he was honored above all his friends.

The Babylonians had an idol called Bel, and there were spent upon him every day twelve great measures of fine flour, forty sheep, and sixty vessels of wine. The King also worshiped him.

The priests and their families had the King to believe that Bel was eating all the food they placed in the temple. The priests would lock the temple, and in the morning all the food was gone. So the next time the priests filled the temple before the King locked the door, Daniel told the King before he locked the door to sprinkle ash over the floor. When he finished, the King locked the temple door.

During the night the priests and their families had a hidden tunnel under the temple, and they would come in and eat and drink all the food. The next morning the King and Daniel went to the temple. When the King unlocked the door, Daniel stopped the King before he entered the temple.

Daniel said, "Look out across the floor." And when the King looked out across the floor, he saw several foot prints, small and large. The King saw how the priests had a hidden entrance to enter the temple and ate all the food. There were seventy priests, their wives and children (Daniel 14th Chapter). Daniel exposed the priests' secret, and the King put them all to death.

Ten Lepers Healed (Luke 17: 10 – 18)

It came to pass when Jesus passed through the midst of Samaria and Galilee, when Jesus entered the village, he met 10 men with the leprosy that stood afar off. They cried out to Jesus saying, "Master, have mercy on us."

When Jesus saw them, he said unto the ten men, "Go, show yourselves to the priest."

As they were on their way, all ten of them were healed. When one saw that he was healed, he turned around and went back and fell down. There he began to glorify God. The Bible said he was a Samaritan.

Now the other nine had to be Jews. Back then the Samaritans did not associate with the Jews. They had a dislike toward each other. Just like what is going on in the world today. Different people hate each other because of their race, culture, religion, and how a person is dressed.

This goes back to the Assyrian conflict. History states that instead of the Samaritans helping the Jews, the Samaritans teamed up with the Assyrians and fought against the Jews. The hate is still going on all around the world, including America. The Samaritan that came back knew the hate that the two groups had toward each other.

The Theme of the 23rd Psalms

This was during the time when the Lord was withdrawing his Spirit from King Saul because of Saul's disobedience. David was one of Saul's commanders, Captain of the Army. When David would go out and fight, he would have victory. Every battle he fought he would win.

Let's go back. David had three brothers that were in King Saul's Army (I Samuel 17:13). They were Eliah, Abinadad and Shammah. Jesse was the father.

David's father called out to David. "David, son, I want you to take a good will package and go see how your brothers are doing."

So David took the good will package to his brothers. When he got to the field, there was a commotion going on. David inquired about the commotion, but his brothers would not tell him. However, one of the soldiers told David about the giant Goliath.

"I will go and fight the giant," David said.

"You're just a lad," the King said.

David began to tell King Saul how he had killed a lion and a bear when they attacked the herds. So, King Saul had David suited up for battle. But all the armor was too heavy for David. The armor was so heavy that David could not move around in it. David picked up 4 to 5 stones and went out to face Goliath. The Bible described Goliath as six cubits and a span (I Samuel 17:4). A span is half of the known number, so Goliath was 9 cubits.

David went before Goliath. Goliath taunted David. David moved to the left, then to the right. Then David put a rock in his sling, targeted Goliath, and killed him.

Now going back when David killed Goliath, the women of the city began to sing a song with lyrics honoring him. "Saul killed his thousand, and David killed 10,000."

King Saul got angry, and went about trying to kill David.

When David wrote the 23rd Psalm, he said, "He prepared a table before me in the presence of my enemy." David was referring to King Saul who had made a feast and had a chair at the feast for David. But David did not go to the feast. King Saul thought he would use this chance to kill David. However, God had a shield of protection around David. King Saul had put out the message that David was trying to kill him. So, King Saul was hunting for David. Twice David could have killed King Saul, but he did not.

King Saul's son, Jonathan, became David's best friend. He kept David on top about what his father had planned.

Back then when a person was King, next in line to the throne would be his son. When Jonathan asked his father what David had done, King Saul got mad at his son and tried to kill him (I Samuel 20 – 33). And the Lord sent an evil spirit upon King Saul (I Samuel 19:9).

Jonathan made a covenant with David (I Samuel 20:16). On the second day of the feast, David did not show up again (I Samuel 20 – 27). That is how the 23rd Psalm was written. David was explaining what had happened to him.

THE FIG TREE
The Forbidden Fruit

Adam and Eve were told not to eat from or touch the tree. The serpent was more subtle than any beast of the field. The serpent tricked Eve. However, Eve told the serpent that tree in the midst of the garden they had instructions from God not to eat from (Genesis 3:1-5).

People have been in limbo about the name of the tree. Some people believe it was an apple tree. Guess what? It wasn't an apple tree. The tree that Adam and Eve ate of was a fig tree.

No sooner than when Adam and Eve ate of the tree, their eyes were open. The Bible said they then realized that they were naked, and sewed fig leaves together to hide their nakedness (Genesis 3 – 7). Adam and Eve had disobeyed the Lord's command.

When Jesus and his disciples were traveling, they came upon a fig tree. Jesus rebuked the fig tree, and it withered and died. People think that the reason why Jesus rebuked the fig tree was because it did not produce fruit. Not so. Jesus could have spoken the word, and the figs would have appeared. Jesus rebuked the fig tree because that was the tree that the Lord told Adam and Eve not to touch or eat from. The Lord knows everything. He knew that Adam and Eve were going to eat of the tree (Matthew 21:18-21).

Now we go to the fig tree (Mark 11:11-13). "When Jesus came to the fig tree, he found nothing but leaves; for the time of figs was not yet." In other words, it wasn't the season for figs to be on the tree. There is a book called *The Lost Books of the Bible* which gives a little more information concerning the fig tree.

YOUR THOUGHTS
—
YOUR OPINIONS

There are different writings on Judas as being James' son, and another as Judas being Simon's son. Could this be a calculated misprint, or was it done on purpose?

Read

1.) Luke 6:16 "Judas, the brother of James and Judas Iscariot, which also was the traitor." This is the same Judas.

2.) John 13:2 "After supper ended, the devil having now put into the heart of Judas Iscariot, Simon's son, to betray him." This was Simon's brother, not his son.

3.) John 6:71 "He spoke of Judas Iscariot, the son of Simon; for he was the one who betrayed him, being one of the twelve." Judas was not Simon's son. He was Simon's brother.

Reference: Matt. 13:55

Goudy Old Style and Algerian on LSI 50# archival white
Type and Design by Karen Paul Stone